BIRDS OF PREY
Red-Tailed
HAWKS

by Melissa Hill

Consulting Editor: Gail Saunders-Smith, PhD

Consultant: Jessica Ehrgott, Bird and Mammal
Trainer, Downtown Aquarium, Denver

CAPSTONE PRESS
a capstone imprint

Pebble Plus is published by Capstone Press,
1710 Roe Crest Drive, North Mankato, Minnesota 56003
www.capstonepub.com

Library of Congress Cataloging-in-Publication Data
Hill, Melissa, 1975–
Red-Tailed Hawks / by Melissa Hill.
pages cm.—(Pebble Plus. Birds of Prey)
Includes bibliographical references and index.
Summary: "Describes the characteristics, habitat, behavior, life cycle, and
threats to red-tailed hawks"—Provided by publisher.
Audience: Ages 5 to 8.
Audience: Grades K to 3.
ISBN 978-1-4914-2093-5 (library binding)
ISBN 978-1-4914-2311-0 (paperback)
ISBN 978-1-4914-2334-9 (eBook PDF)
1. Red-tailed hawk—Juvenile literature. I. Title.
QL696.F32H554 2014
598.9'44—dc23   2014032783

5545 5496 01/15

Editorial Credits
Jeni Wittrock, editor; Peggie Carley and Janet Kusmierski, designers;
Svetlana Zhurkin, media researcher; Katy LaVigne, production specialist

Photo Credits
Alamy: Johann Schumacher, 13; Dreamstime: Bruce Macqueen, 21, Paul Roedding, 5,
Petar Kremenarov, 9; Getty Images: UIG/Auscape, 15; iStockphotos: Dantesattic, 7,
iculizard, cover, back cover, Ronald Walker, 17; Nicole Meyer, 1; Shutterstock:
balounm, back cover (background), Paul Reeves Photography, 19, Ronnie Howard, 11

Note to Parents and Teachers

The Birds of Prey set supports national science standards related
to life science. This book describes and illustrates red-tailed hawks.
The images support early readers in understanding the text. The
repetition of words and phrases helps early readers learn new
words. This book also introduces early readers to subject-specific
vocabulary words, which are defined in the Glossary section. Early
readers may need assistance to read some words and to use the
Table of Contents, Glossary, Read More, Internet Sites, Critical
Thinking Using the Common Core, and Index sections of the book.

Printed in the United States of America in Stevens Point, Wisconsin
102014   008479WZS15

Table of Contents

Living Free

High above, a hawk circles in the wind. From below, its white belly and red tail feathers show. Red-tailed hawks can soar for hours.

Red-tailed hawks live in North and Central America. They are found in many habitats. Deserts, fields, and other open spaces are their favorites.

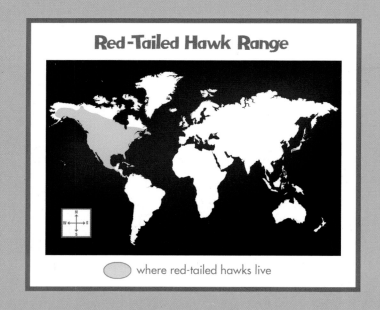

Red-Tailed Hawk Range

where red-tailed hawks live

Hunting Hawk

Hunting red-tails can spot prey 1,000 feet (305 meters) away. Mice, squirrels, rabbits, snakes, and birds are on the menu.

From high above, a red-tail spots prey. It dives toward its meal. The hawk grabs its prey with its sharp talons.

talon

Red-Tail Families

In spring, red-tailed hawks build large nests out of sticks. The same hawks may use the nest for 10 years or more.

Red-tailed hawks raise two to four chicks each year. When they hatch, chicks are covered in downy feathers.

Red-tail chicks grow quickly.
Around 42 days after hatching,
they begin to fly. They may live
for 20 years.

Dangers and Helpers

Red-tailed hawks face dangers.

Some red-tails are hunted

by great horned owls.

Others are hit by cars

or eat poisoned prey.

Each year red-tails may eat thousands of rodents. Thanks to red-tails, fewer animals eat our crops and gardens. Red-tailed hawks are helpful birds.

Glossary

downy—soft and fuzzy

habitat—a type of place where an animal is usually found

hatch—to break out of an egg

poison—a substance that can harm or kill

prey—an animal that is hunted by another animal for food

rodent—one of a group of furry animals with teeth made for chewing

soar—to fly high in the air

talon—a sharp, curved claw

Read More

Martin, Isabel. *Birds: A Question and Answer Book.* Animal Kingdom Questions and Answers. North Mankato, Minn.: Capstone Press, 2015.

McCarthy, Meghan. *City Hawk: The Story of Pale Male.* New York: Simon and Schuster Books for Young Readers, 2007.

Schuetz, Kari. *Hawks.* Backyard Wildlife. Minneapolis: Bellwether Media, Inc., 2014.

Internet Sites

FactHound offers a safe, fun way to find Internet sites related to this book. All of the sites on FactHound have been researched by our staff.

Here's all you do:

Visit *www.facthound.com*

Type in this code: 9781491420935

Super-cool stuff! Check out projects, games and lots more at www.capstonekids.com

Critical Thinking Using the Common Core

Why are red-tailed hawks helpful to gardens?
(Key Ideas and Details)

If many farmers use poison to kill rodents in their fields,
what might happen to red-tailed hawks?
(Integration of Knowledge and Ideas)

Index

Word Count: 191
Grade: 1
Early-Intervention Level: 14